LIVE OR DIE?

SURVIVAL CHALLENGE

WARNING WARNING WARNING WA

WARNING WARNING WARNING W

WARNING WARN WARNING WA

WARNING WARN WARNING

WARN WARNING WARNING WA

WARNING WARNING

ARNING WARNING

PAT SHAND

TABLE OF CONTENTS

CAN YOU SURVIVE THE CHALLENGE?

The world is a fascinating place, filled with great beauty and great danger to match. Take a journey with us into the wild, where we will encounter some of the most mesmerizing animals and the most perilous natural disasters, as well as situations that will challenge your basic instincts. From cougar attacks to jellyfish stings, from blizzards to tsunamis, and from house fires to quicksand, we will face off with death, and armed with our knowledge, our instincts, and the power of our will to survive . . . we'll see who makes it out alive.

WELCOME TO THE SURVIVAL CHALLENGE!

GRIZZLY BEAR ENCOUNTER!

THERE IS SO MUCH TO ENJOY IN THE GREAT OUTDOORS, AND ONE OF THE BEST WAYS TO EXPERIENCE NATURE IS HIKING. HOWEVER, NATURE CAN ALSO BE TREACHEROUS. ONE OF A HIKER'S WORST NIGHTMARES IS ENCOUNTERING A GRIZZLY. THESE BEARS CAN WEIGH 800 POUNDS (360 KG) AND STAND UP TO EIGHT FEET TALL. EVEN THOUGH THEIR DIET IS LIMITED PRIMARILY TO FRUITS, NUTS, AND SMALL ANIMALS, THEIR SIZE MAKES THEM DANGEROUS TO HUMANS.

FACT!

Grizzlies are a subspecies of brown bear, also known as the silvertip bear.

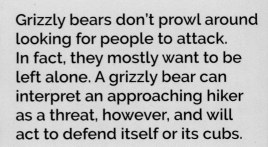

Grizzly bears don't prowl around looking for people to attack. In fact, they mostly want to be left alone. A grizzly bear can interpret an approaching hiker as a threat, however, and will act to defend itself or its cubs.

LIVE OR DIE?

An eight-foot-tall grizzly bear is approaching you. It has you in its sights and there is nowhere to hide. Your immediate reaction is panic, but you have to push past the crippling terror if you hope to survive! It's time to act.

WHAT WOULD YOU DO?

OPTION #1

MAKE NOISE BY YELLING, BANGING, AND STOMPING.

OPTION #2

SLOWLY RETREAT, SHOWING THE BEAR THAT YOU ARE NOT A THREAT.

OPTION #3

RUN AWAY AS QUICKLY AS HUMANLY POSSIBLE.

SUCCESS! OPTION #2

By moving slowly and keeping your eyes on the bear, you are able to show this startled grizzly that you aren't a threat. Though this method isn't foolproof—especially when you have encountered an agitated mama bear attempting to protect her young—it is the best and most effective way to diffuse this dangerous situation. If this fails, bear spray can help as well.

CAUTION! OPTION #1

Making a bunch of noise works with other species of bears, such as the black bear, which is easily scared away. This sort of maneuver will not have the same effect on a grizzly bear. Instead, the grizzly will see you as an even greater (and more annoying) threat.

DANGER! OPTION #3

Unfortunately, "as quickly as humanly possible" isn't quick enough. Running will trigger the grizzly bear to give chase, and that won't work out for you.

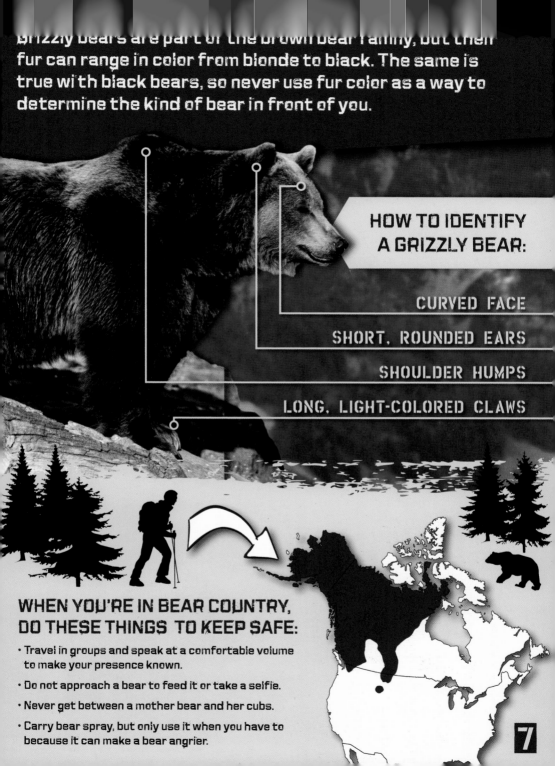

grizzly bears are part of the brown bear family, but their fur can range in color from blonde to black. The same is true with black bears, so never use fur color as a way to determine the kind of bear in front of you.

HOW TO IDENTIFY A GRIZZLY BEAR:

CURVED FACE

SHORT, ROUNDED EARS

SHOULDER HUMPS

LONG, LIGHT-COLORED CLAWS

WHEN YOU'RE IN BEAR COUNTRY, DO THESE THINGS TO KEEP SAFE:

- Travel in groups and speak at a comfortable volume to make your presence known.

- Do not approach a bear to feed it or take a selfie.

- Never get between a mother bear and her cubs.

- Carry bear spray, but only use it when you have to because it can make a bear angrier.

TORNADO!

A TORNADO, ALSO KNOWN AS A TWISTER OR A CYCLONE, IS ONE OF THE MOST VIOLENT TYPES OF STORMS. APPEARING AS A SPINNING FUNNEL OF CLOUDS, THE MOST INTENSE TWISTERS CAN REACH SPEEDS IN EXCESS OF 300 MILES PER HOUR, LEAVING DESTRUCTION IN THEIR PATH. WHILE METEOROLOGISTS ARE SOMETIMES ABLE TO PUT AT-RISK AREAS ON ALERT, TORNADOES ARE KNOWN TO FORM QUICKLY, RENDERING IT IMPOSSIBLE FOR THE AFFECTED NEIGHBORHOODS TO RECEIVE WARNING.

FACT!

Tornadoes often spawn from tropical storms, occurring when a warm front meets a cold front.

Tornadoes have been known to leave paths of damage as long as 50 miles. Because of the level of devastation these storms reach, twisters have been the subject of many Hollywood blockbuster movies.

LIVE OR DIE?

A storm has hit your neighborhood, and spawned a tornado. You are with your family at home, and you have a car, which leaves you with multiple options.

It is time to assess the situation and decide the best course of action.

OPTION #1

GET YOUR FAMILY INTO THE CAR AND HEAD AWAY FROM THE STORM.

OPTION #2

STAY INSIDE, KEEPING AN EYE ON THE STORM THROUGH THE WINDOW SO YOU KNOW IF THE TORNADO IS APPROACHING.

OPTION #3

HUNKER DOWN IN YOUR BASEMENT OR STORM SHELTER.

SUCCESS! OPTION #3

Taking shelter as far underground as you can manage is your best bet, as you have now put as many layers of protection between yourself and the storm as possible. To make yourself even safer, protect your head with a helmet and be sure to wear sturdy shoes in case there is broken glass.

CAUTION! OPTION #2

It is better to be inside than outside during a tornado, but you don't want to be anywhere near a window. There is little you can do to reinforce the glass during such a storm. Even if the tornado doesn't hit your home, the winds and perhaps even hail could shatter the glass.

DANGER! OPTION #1

Though your instincts might scream for you to get as far away from the tornado as possible, you don't want to lose the protection that your home offers. Twisters can change direction without warning, and your path away from the storm might suddenly be directly in the danger zone.

The Fujita scale is a system designed to classify a tornado by its level of intensity. The weakest tornadoes register as a F0, and the most intense register as F5.

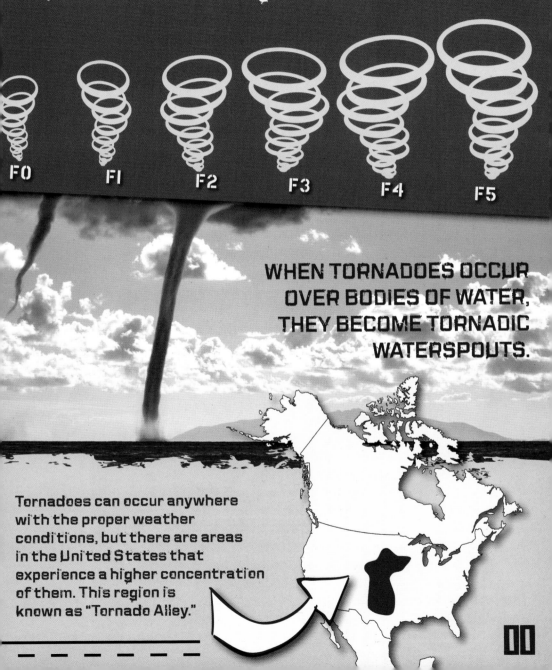

F0

F1

F2

F3

F4

F5

WHEN TORNADOES OCCUR OVER BODIES OF WATER, THEY BECOME TORNADIC WATERSPOUTS.

Tornadoes can occur anywhere with the proper weather conditions, but there are areas in the United States that experience a higher concentration of them. This region is known as "Tornado Alley."

AVALANCHE!

SKIING DOWN A SNOWY HILL MIGHT BE AS CLOSE AS A PERSON CAN GET TO FEELING WHAT IT'S LIKE TO FLY. BUT THAT GLORIOUS SENSATION CAN BE CUT DEVASTATINGLY SHORT BY A SUDDEN AVALANCHE. AS THIS MASS OF SNOW, ICE, AND SOMETIMES ROCKS FALLS RAPIDLY DOWN THE SLOPE, IT PICKS UP SPEED, CREATING AN EXTREME HAZARD FOR SKIERS BELOW.

FACT!

Suffocation, bodily injuries, asphyxia, and hypothermia are the most common causes of fatalities in the event of an avalanche.

There are many events that can trigger an avalanche, such as changes in temperature, heavy accumulation of new snow or rain, and earthquakes. Avalanches can also occur due to events called "artificial triggers." These include loud sounds, such as a gunshot, or a disruption in a build-up of snow by a skier.

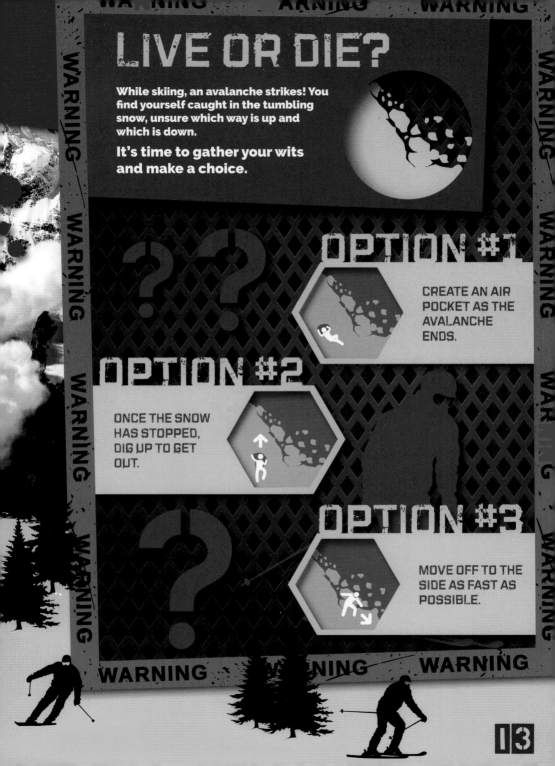

LIVE OR DIE?

While skiing, an avalanche strikes! You find yourself caught in the tumbling snow, unsure which way is up and which is down.

It's time to gather your wits and make a choice.

OPTION #1

CREATE AN AIR POCKET AS THE AVALANCHE ENDS.

OPTION #2

ONCE THE SNOW HAS STOPPED, DIG UP TO GET OUT.

OPTION #3

MOVE OFF TO THE SIDE AS FAST AS POSSIBLE.

13

SUCCESS! OPTION #3

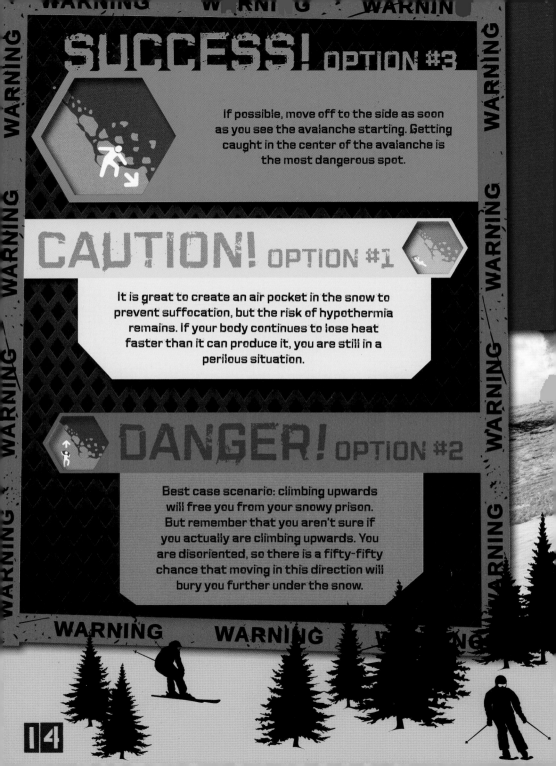

If possible, move off to the side as soon as you see the avalanche starting. Getting caught in the center of the avalanche is the most dangerous spot.

CAUTION! OPTION #1

It is great to create an air pocket in the snow to prevent suffocation, but the risk of hypothermia remains. If your body continues to lose heat faster than it can produce it, you are still in a perilous situation.

DANGER! OPTION #2

Best case scenario: climbing upwards will free you from your snowy prison. But remember that you aren't sure if you actually are climbing upwards. You are disoriented, so there is a fifty-fifty chance that moving in this direction will bury you further under the snow.

TYPES OF AVALANCHES:

LOOSE SNOW AVALANCHES, also known as slough or sluff, start with loose snow at a single point. They can grow very large as they move at speeds upwards of 40 mph (64.3 kmh).

AIRBORNE POWDER AVALANCHES develop when the loose snow avalanches increase in speed beyond 40 mph and the snow is moving powerfully enough to take to the air. These highly destructive avalanches can race down a mountain as fast as 175 mph (280 kmh).

SLAB AVALANCHES occur when heavily packed snow breaks away and slides down a mountain in one large piece. Hard slabs can happen when the wind is very strong and the snow is tightly packed. Soft slabs don't need heavy wind and they usually break up into powdery snow as they go downhill.

WET AVALANCHES are common when the weather starts to get warm and the snow begins to thaw in springtime. They can form either as loose snow or slab avalanches and travel at any speed.

ICE AVALANCHES occur when large sheets of ice break off a mountain.

FACT!
Hypothermia begins when your body temperature falls under 95 degrees.

15

SNAKE BITE!

NOT ALL SNAKE BITES HAVE THE POTENTIAL TO BE FATAL, AS NOT ALL SNAKES ARE VENOMOUS. HOWEVER, 15 PERCENT OF SNAKES ARE INDEED CONSIDERED DANGEROUS TO HUMANS, WITH THE MAJORITY OF MEDICAL ISSUES ARISING FROM THIS THREATENING TRIO OF SNAKES: COBRAS, VIPERS, AND KRAITS. ENCOUNTERING A VENOMOUS SNAKE IN THE WILD CAN BE A TERRIFYING EVENT BECAUSE, LIKE GRIZZLY BEARS, THESE CREATURES WILL ATTACK HUMANS WITHOUT HESITATION IF THEY FEEL THREATENED.

FACT!

Even venomous snakes do not always inject their victims with venom upon biting them. These are known as "dry bites."

The area in which a snake bites a person can determine if the attack is life-threatening or not. While a superficial bite will likely not be fatal, a deeper bite to the abdomen is far more dangerous. The classification of the dangerous nature of venomous snake bites varies based on species and region

SUCCESS! OPTION #3

If you do not have a snake bite kit handy, your best course of action is to call for emergency help. In order to provide the best information and receive the best care, be sure to note the color of the snake, as well as any other possible physical markers. Treatment will vary based on species. While you wait for help to arrive, be sure to not exert yourself or consume any liquids or foods.

CAUTION! OPTION #1

It is understandable to think it would be best to remove the venom from the wound, but doing it with your mouth would be dangerous. A suction device of any kind, often found in snake bite kits, would do this more effeciently and safely than your mouth.

DANGER! OPTION #2

Applying a tourniquet to the arm could possibly result in the limb requiring amputation. Avoid this at all costs. Avoid applying ice to the wound as well.

SNAKES CAN BE FOUND WORLDWIDE, ON
EVERY CONTINENT EXCEPT ANTARCTICA.

Ilha da Queimada Grande is a land mass off the coast of Brazil more commonly known as "Snake Island." The island is so covered in these slithery reptiles that there are said to be up to five snakes per every square yard on the island.

About 7,000 venomous snake bites are reported in the United States each year, with only six fatalities on average. Other parts of the world have much more venomous snakes, with India reporting around 11,000 deaths from snake bites a year.

7,000 BITES

STUCK IN A BURNING BUILDING!

IT IS SAFE TO SAY THAT THE IDEA OF WAKING UP TO DISCOVER THAT YOUR HOUSE IS ON FIRE IS AMONG ANYONE'S WORST NIGHTMARES. THERE ARE APPROXIMATELY 365,000 HOUSE FIRES PER YEAR, WITH ABOUT 3,000 CIVILIAN DEATHS AND 11,000 CIVILIAN INJURIES. THE ORIGIN POINT OF HOUSE FIRES IS MOST COMMONLY THE KITCHEN.

FACT!

More people die due to smoke inhalation during a house fire than being burned by flames.

20

Two out of every five home fires start in the kitchen. This is sometimes a result of leaving food unattended while it cooks, but the most common incident is a grease fire, which results from frying. Though kitchen fires are the leading cause of injuries in home fires, statistically, smoking-related fires are known to be more fatal, and are the leading cause of fire-related deaths.

LIVE OR DIE?

You wake up to a raging fire, seemingly trapped in your home. Smoke is rolling into your room, replacing the oxygen with poison. As you witness your house going up in flames, you have to act quickly, or it will be too late to save yourself.

What do you do?

OPTION #1

KEEP LOW, CRAWLING ON YOUR HANDS AND KNEES PAST THE FIRE AND TO YOUR EXIT.

OPTION #2

ATTEMPT TO EXTINGUISH THE FIRE.

OPTION #3

STAY IN YOUR ROOM AND CLOSE THE DOOR TO PREVENT THE FIRE FROM GETTING TO YOU.

WARNING WARNING WARNING

21

SUCCESS! OPTION #1

Smoke rises, so the best thing that you can do is stay close to the ground as you attempt to exit. Make your way toward a door leading outside or, if that isn't possible, a window.

CAUTION! OPTION #2

You might want to protect your home, but attempting to extinguish a fire that has already reached dangerous levels may put your life in jeopardy. Stick to your exit plan, but if flames block all of your exits, find the safest room and yell loudly for help.

DANGER! OPTION #3

Even if the fire has not yet gotten to your room, closing the door as you wait for help will not prevent the smoke from making its way under your door . . . and remember, the noxious smoke is even more dangerous than the flames themselves!

If you are trapped in a room and the door or doorknob is hot, stay where you are because the fire is on the other side. Block the bottom of the door with wet towels if you can and wait for rescue. This will prevent smoke from entering the room, extending your likelihood of survival.

THE BEST WAY TO SURVIVE A HOUSE FIRE IS FOR YOUR FAMILY TO HAVE A PLAN IN PLACE BEFORE THE FIRE HAPPENS.

- Ask your parents if you have smoke detectors and if they're working properly.
- Choose a window that would make a good exit if doors are blocked. Try to come up with at least two exits from every room.
- Draw a map of possible escape routes and keep it handy.
- Designate a spot outside the house for the family to meet once everyone is out.
- Practice fire drills with your family.

SINKING IN QUICKSAND!

NATURE CAN POSE MANY DANGERS TO HIKERS. THESE MENACES ARE NOT LIMITED TO AN AGITATED WILD ANIMAL ATTEMPTING TO PROTECT ITSELF. SOMETIMES, THE TERRAIN ITSELF CAN BECOME A DEADLY THREAT. QUICKSAND IS CREATED WHEN SAND, SILT, OR CLAY BECOMES SATURATED WITH WATER OR SUBJECTED TO AN EARTHQUAKE. THIS SOIL, WHICH TAKES ON HIGH LEVELS OF VISCOSITY (STICKINESS) DUE TO INTERNAL FRICTION (MOTION), WILL SEEMINGLY PULL AT THOSE WHO HAVE SET FOOT IN IT DOWN INTO ITS MUDDY PITS.

FACT!

Quicksand occurs most often around riverbanks and marshes, but it can appear almost anywhere, including deserts.

DANGER

QUICKSAND STAY AWAY

Though movies and television have depicted quicksand as almost a living creature attempting to swallow its victims whole, these pits are often no more than a few feet deep. The quicksand itself doesn't create a suction effect, but rather the weight of the victim as well as sudden movements will cause those caught in the pits to sink deeper.

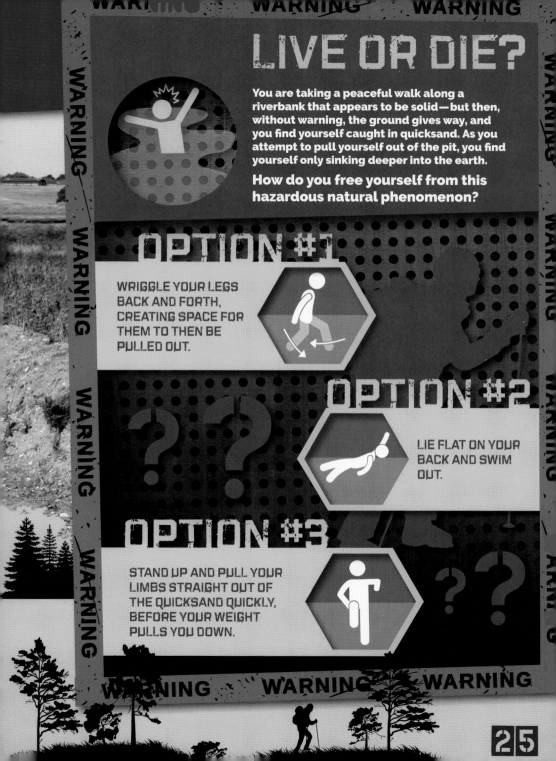

LIVE OR DIE?

You are taking a peaceful walk along a riverbank that appears to be solid—but then, without warning, the ground gives way, and you find yourself caught in quicksand. As you attempt to pull yourself out of the pit, you find yourself only sinking deeper into the earth.

How do you free yourself from this hazardous natural phenomenon?

OPTION #1

WRIGGLE YOUR LEGS BACK AND FORTH, CREATING SPACE FOR THEM TO THEN BE PULLED OUT.

OPTION #2

LIE FLAT ON YOUR BACK AND SWIM OUT.

OPTION #3

STAND UP AND PULL YOUR LIMBS STRAIGHT OUT OF THE QUICKSAND QUICKLY, BEFORE YOUR WEIGHT PULLS YOU DOWN.

25

SUCCESS! OPTION #2

Despite common misconceptions—mostly due to the depiction of quicksand in action movies—the safest way to free yourself from quicksand is to get onto your back and carefully, slowly swim out. Though the pit is thick, you will most likely be able to float to a safe level, at which point you will ultimately be able to free yourself.

CAUTION! OPTION #1

Though creating space for your limbs to be withdrawn is safer than thrashing around, sudden movements can still dig you deeper into the quicksand. If you are unable to get directly onto your back, slowly but surely creating space for your limbs to move may be a good way to put yourself in a position to carry out the effective method of Option #2.

DANGER! OPTION #3

Freeing your legs is key, but attempting to pull them straight out of the quicksand will only cause you to sink deeper. It is also important to remain calm and make slow, purposeful movements, as quick actions and thrashing are guaranteed to put you in a far worse situation.

WARNING WARNING WARNING

It is unlikely that quicksand pits are deep enough for you to find yourself completely submerged, but if you are unable to free yourself from the pit, you will find yourself vulnerable to wildlife, high tide, or other dangerous elements.

WAYS TO AVOID QUICKSAND:

- Keep an eye out around wet terrain near riverbanks, lakes, swamps, marshes, and other places where water meets land. Be extra cautious after heavy rainstorms.

- If water is bubbling up from below the ground, watch out. If the ground is rippled, that might also be a sign.

- Watch your step by tapping the ground in front of you with a stick. If the dirt gives way from the pressure of the stick, take another path.

LOST IN THE WOODS!

ALL AROUND THE WORLD, CAMPERS HAVE ENJOYED GETTING IN TOUCH WITH THEIR ENVIRONMENT BY HIKING THROUGH THE WOODS. HOWEVER, FROM A WRONG TURN OR A FAULTY MAP TO A TRAIL BLOWN AWAY BY HARSH WINDS, THERE ARE COUNTLESS WAYS TO GET LOST. UP TO 2,000 PEOPLE OF ALL AGES GET LOST IN THE WOODS EVERY YEAR. IN THESE CASES, SURVIVAL OFTEN DEPENDS ON HOW MUCH THE HIKER HAS PREPARED FOR THIS EXACT CIRCUMSTANCE.

FACT!

Though many of the berries you will find in the woods are poisonous, edible fruits such as blueberries, blackberries, raspberries, honeysuckle berries, and others are safe to eat if properly and thoroughly identified.

Depending on where you are located in the world, the species of animals and assortment of vegetation you will encounter in the woods vary greatly. Some of the more harmless wildlife includes beavers and owls, but bobcats, bears, and coyotes can be found in certain locations as well.

LIVE OR DIE?

You have taken a wrong turn, and you can't seem to place yourself on your map of the woods. Disoriented by the seemingly endless trees sprawled out in every direction, you begin to worry that you will not make it back to your campground before night falls. As you begin to lose daylight, your hope dwindles along with it. You must assess your situation and apply everything you've learned about survival in the woods.

What do you do to get yourself back to civilization?

OPTION #1

RUN IN ONE DIRECTION, ATTEMPTING TO BEAT OUT THE SUNSET.

OPTION #2

MOVE DOWNHILL TO FIND WATER.

OPTION #3

STAY WHERE YOU ARE AND WAIT FOR RESCUE.

SUCCESS! OPTION #3

If you've told someone where you're hiking, the safest option is to find a spot to rest and wait. Moving further into the woods will only make it harder for a search party to find you.

CAUTION! OPTION #2

Moving downhill is another option because that is the direction water flows, and keeping hydrated is essential to survival. If you find a water supply, stay in that spot to wait for rescue. Just don't waste too much energy in your search.

DANGER! OPTION #1

Running in any direction will expend a great deal of energy, and can possibly lead to an injury. When lost in the woods, it might seem as if you are racing against dusk, but your chief concerns should be conserving energy and keeping your strength.

When hiking in the woods, always tell someone where you are going. That will increase your chances of being rescued.

HIKING TIPS:

- Pack lightly. The heaviest things you should carry while hiking are food and water.

- Don't over do it. If you can walk and talk without huffing and puffing, you're moving at a good speed.

- If it's a long hike, take a 10 minute break every hour you're walking.

- Unless your path is a circle, remember you have to walk back. Don't exhaust yourself going in one direction.

- Keep an eye on the sun. Don't start your hike too late in the day.

SHARK ATTACK!

THERE IS NOTHING MORE TERRIFYING TO SWIMMERS THAN THAT CLASSIC IMAGE OF A SHARK FIN PROTRUDING FROM THE WATER. MANY SPECIES OF SHARKS ARE CONSIDERED APEX PREDATORS, PLACING THEM AT THE TOP OF THE AQUATIC FOOD CHAIN. THOUGH ONLY A FEW SPECIES OF SHARKS ARE KNOWN TO LASH OUT AT HUMANS IN UNPROVOKED ATTACKS, THESE POWERFUL CREATURES HAVE GARNERED A DEADLY REPUTATION AS MAN-EATERS.

FACT!

There is evidence of sharks dating back 400 million years, which means that these resilient creatures have survived five extinction-level events.

There are over 400 species of sharks, but only three—the great white shark, the tiger shark, and the bull shark—are popularly known for their unprovoked aggression toward humans. The endangered oceanic white tip sharks are known as the deadliest sharks of all, but mostly due to preying on shipwrecks for food rather than purely for aggression. Hammerheads are commonly known as fearsome sharks, but humans prove to be more of a threat to the shark than the shark is to humans.

LIVE OR DIE?

On a casual swim through seemingly calm waters, you see the dorsal fin cutting through the water. It is too close for you to make it safely back to land. Panic floods your chest as the shark circles around you, preparing for its attack.

What would you do?

OPTION #1

STRIKE THE SHARK ON THE NOSE.

OPTION #2

MOVE WITH THE SHARK TO DIRECTLY FACE IT AT ALL TIMES, SPREADING YOUR LIMBS TO APPEAR TO BE A LARGER THREAT.

OPTION #3

PLAY DEAD.

SUCCESS! OPTION #2

Though no method of defending yourself from a shark is 100 percent successful, directly facing the shark and calmly spreading your limbs will communicate to the predator that you are a larger threat than originally thought. Because of the physical strength that sharks possess, the safest way to survive a possible attack is to diffuse the situation before the first strike.

CAUTION! OPTION #1

The danger in battling a shark is obvious, but if one attacks, your only recourse is to physically defend yourself. Theories about striking the shark on the nose vary, so your best bet is to attack the shark where it is most vulnerable, including its gills and especially its eyes. If you are able to injure its eyes, your likelihood of survival is increased.

DANGER! OPTION #3

Sharks will go for easy prey, so this trick won't do. Conversely, neither will thrashing and making noise in attempt to scare it away. Calm, purposeful action is key.

Though pop culture paints sharks as terrifying monsters, more often than not, the biggest sharks are the most harmless, sustaining themselves on plankton rather than unsuspecting swimmers.

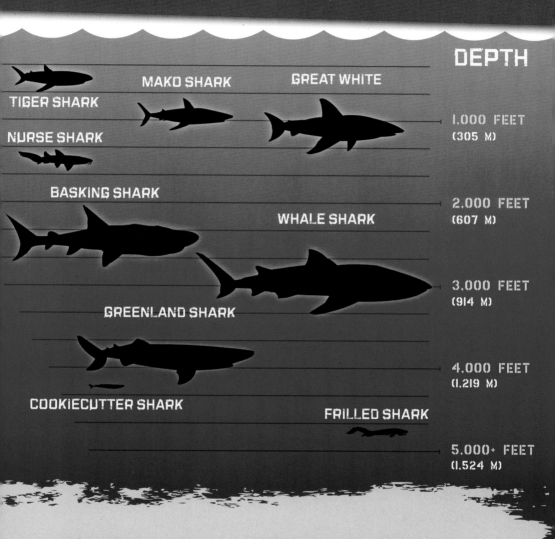

DEPTH

TIGER SHARK

MAKO SHARK

GREAT WHITE

NURSE SHARK

1,000 FEET
(305 M)

BASKING SHARK

WHALE SHARK

2,000 FEET
(607 M)

3,000 FEET
(914 M)

GREENLAND SHARK

4,000 FEET
(1,219 M)

COOKIECUTTER SHARK

FRILLED SHARK

5,000+ FEET
(1,524 M)

SHARKS LIVE IN THE OCEAN AT ALL DIFFERENT DEPTHS. SOME CAN SWIM AT THE DEEPEST, DARKEST DEPTHS, WHILE OTHERS STAY CLOSER TO THE TOP AND CAN SWIM CLOSE TO SHORE.

ADRIFT AT SEA!

TRAVELING BY SEA CAN BE ONE OF THE MOST INTERESTING MEANS OF TRANSPORTATION. CRUISE SHIPS HAVE PROVIDED ENTERTAINMENT AND ADVENTURE FOR PEOPLE IN NEED OF ESCAPE; FISHING BOATS ARE ESSENTIAL FOR MANY COMMERCIAL ENTERPRISES; AND PLEASURE BOATS HAVE BEEN THE SUBJECT OF FASCINATION FOR THOSE INTERESTED IN SPORTS AND LEISURE. WHY, SOME PEOPLE HAVE EVEN MADE BOATS INTO THEIR HOMES! HOWEVER, BOATS TRAVELING LONG DISTANCES ARE VULNERABLE TO STORMS AND HAVE, IN SEVERE SITUATIONS, BEEN SHIPWRECKED, LEAVING THEIR OCCUPANTS ADRIFT AT SEA.

FACT!

Larger vessels are referred to as ships, while smaller vessels are known as boats.

Shipwrecks can happen as a result of onboard difficulties such as fire, explosion, or technical malfunctions, as well as external threats such as storms or collisions. In modern times, shipwrecks due to these circumstances have declined due to advances in technology.

LIVE OR DIE?

A violent storm has led to your small boat's destruction. As the boat breaks apart, you find yourself submerged in the cold water. You manage to break the surface of the water, but as you take stock of your surroundings, there is no sign of land.

You are adrift at sea . . . how do you survive?

OPTION #1

BEGIN SWIMMING AS QUICKLY AS POSSIBLE IN THE DIRECTION YOU LAST SAW LAND WHILE ON YOUR BOAT.

OPTION #2

TAKE STOCK OF YOUR SURROUNDINGS AND CREATE A PLAN BASED ON WHAT YOU HAVE.

OPTION #3

SCREAM FOR HELP.

SUCCESS! OPTION #2

First and foremost, your survival will depend on your initial reaction. Before acting, take stock of your surroundings. Can you use parts of your boat as flotation devices? Are there multiple life vests floating in the water? Is there any spare food or water that hasn't been damaged in the shipwreck? Can any of the debris be used as a weapon? Can any of these items help you signal for help once you make it to land? After asking yourself these questions, you can assemble the tools that will be helpful and begin to make your way in the direction of land.

DANGER! OPTION #1

With no concrete information regarding the whereabouts of land, you do not want to expend energy by rapidly swimming back in the direction you think you came from. Wits are more important than speed in this situation.

DANGER! OPTION #3

If the water is calm, you'll be able to see pretty far, so yelling for a boat that isn't in sight will only waste energy.

If you are able to identify a problem with your craft before it is shipwrecked, the first priority is always to find the source of any leak and plug it.

It would be great if you could swim to a populated beach to be rescued, but here's what you do if you find yourself on an uninhabited island:

- Find a clean water supply.
- Build shelter. (It can be very basic. It just needs to protect you from the elements.)
- Search for food.
- Start a fire for signaling and for warmth.
- Arrange rocks on the beach in an X to alert a search party to your location.

FALLING THROUGH ICE!

ICE SKATING ON A FROZEN POND CAN BE GREAT FUN IN WINTER, BUT IF THE WATER ISN'T FULLY FROZEN, PEOPLE PLAYING ON THE ICE MIGHT FIND THEMSELVES IN A DEADLY SITUATION. SOMETIMES, PEOPLE CONSCIOUSLY CHOOSE TO WALK OUT ONTO THIN ICE FOR SPORT, EVEN THOUGH THEY KNOW THE DANGER! WHETHER YOU ARE ICE FISHING OR THRILL SEEKING, OR EVEN WALKING ONTO ICE AS A SEEMINGLY INNOCENT DARE, FALLING THROUGH THIN ICE CAN BE FATAL.

FACT!

Ice needs to be at least four inches (10.2 cm) thick before it's considered safe for people to walk on.

When a human is submerged in freezing water, it generally takes them 15 minutes to lose consciousness, and 45 minutes to die. Hypothermia sets in very quickly, and its effects will limit the mobility of the person exposed to these extreme conditions.

LIVE OR DIE?

It is the dead of winter and the lake in front of you has been frozen for many days, so you think it's safe to cross. As you take your first tentative step out, you become confident upon feeling the sturdiness of the ice. However, after just a few more steps toward the center of the lake, you hear a sharp crack. Before you can take a step backward, the ice splits under you and you are submerged in water so cold that it feels as if your whole body is screaming.

What do you do?

OPTION #1

RUSH TO THE SURFACE, GRAB ONTO THE ICE, PULL YOURSELF OUT, AND SLIDE ON YOUR FEET BACK TO SAFETY.

OPTION #2

SWIM TO THE SURFACE, GRAB ONTO THE ICE, KICK YOUR FEET TO PROPEL YOURSELF OUT, AND ROLL ACROSS THE ICE TO SAFETY.

OPTION #3

SWIM TO THE SURFACE AND STRIKE THE ICE FROM BELOW, CREATING AN IMMEDIATE HOLE FROM WHICH YOU CAN EMERGE.

SUCCESS! OPTION #2

Your top priority is to get to the surface, but the way you carry out this goal will determine if you survive. When you emerge from the water and grab onto the ice, the sudden pressure of your body weight may crack off the layer of ice you are attempting to use for leverage. Instead of putting pressure on the ice, kick your feet to propel yourself horizontally onto the ice. Once you are there, roll across the ice to evenly distribute your weight.

CAUTION! OPTION #3

This option may work if you are unable to navigate back to the hole you initially fell through, but it poses possible danger if you find yourself below a thicker area of the ice. Though it is natural to panic in this situation, you greatly increase your chance of survival by finding the initial hole and carrying out Option #2.

DANGER! OPTION #1

It is understandable and instinctual to attempt to stand up on the ice so that you can make it off the perilous lake as quickly as possible, but putting your body weight on such a focused area can create a bigger hole or even open up a new hole in the ice.

Once safe, though it seems counterproductive, you will want to remove your waterlogged clothing as quickly as possible. Heading to a source of heat is important, but the freezing water soaked into your clothing can counteract the heat if not taken off.

People who have been exposed to freezing water for extended periods of time are vulnerable to hypothermia and frostbite. Frostbite is classified in degrees (first, second, third, and fourth), with the most extreme frostbite necessitating amputation of affected limbs.

Warning signs for hypothermia include shivering, dizziness, confusion, rapid breathing or heart rate, and difficulty speaking.

EARTHQUAKE!

IT'S TRUE THAT SOME AREAS ARE MORE PRONE TO EARTHQUAKES, BUT THE SHIFTING OF ROCKS IN THE EARTH'S CRUST CAN CAUSE THESE PHENOMENA TO HAPPEN ANYTIME, ANYWHERE. MANY EARTHQUAKES HAPPEN EACH DAY—APPROXIMATELY 50—WITH VARYING LEVELS OF INTENSITY. SOMETIMES, EARTHQUAKES ARE SO MILD THAT THEY CANNOT BE FELT, WHILE OTHER TIMES, THEY CAN RESULT IN WIDESPREAD DAMAGE AND DEATH.

Over 13,000 people die in earthquakes every year, with an annual average of almost five million people affected by these natural disasters. In some cases, earthquakes can trigger tsunamis, avalanches, and fires, exponentially increasing the level of devastation.

LIVE OR DIE?

You are at home when the ground begins to shake. Books are falling off shelves, glasses are sliding out of the cabinet and shattering on the ground, and you have to get to safety.

As the intensity of the earthquake increases, what do you do?

OPTION #1

TAKE COVER UNDER YOUR DOORWAY.

OPTION #2

RUN OUTSIDE.

OPTION #3

DROP TO THE GROUND AND TAKE COVER UNDER SOMETHING STURDY.

45

SUCCESS! OPTION #3

Just like you would in the event of a tornado, staying close to the ground and protected from falling debris will help you survive. Be sure, though, that you aren't taking cover under something that could collapse during the earthquake.

DANGER! OPTION #1

This used to be an effective method of surviving earthquakes back when the doorways in the average home were far sturdier than the rest of the house. Now, homes are more reinforced, so you are no more likely to be protected under a doorway than you are in any other part of your home. If your door has any glass in it, this can be a dangerous option.

DANGER! OPTION #2

Stay where you are. You can easily be knocked off your feet if you try to run during a violent earthquake. Exterior walls are also more likely to collapse than interior walls, so you'd be moving toward a more dangerous part of the building if you head for the exit.

THE LARGEST EARTHQUAKE IN THE WORLD,
DUBBED THE "GREAT CHILEAN EARTHQUAKE,"
WAS CLASSIFIED AS A STUNNING
9.5 ON THE RICHTER MAGNITUDE SCALE.

AFTER THE SHOCK

Just because an earthquake is over, doesn't mean the danger has passed. Once the shaking stops, you or your parents should do the following:

- Make sure you (and the people around you) haven't been injured.
- If your home has suffered serious damage, get out.
- Watch out for broken glass and debris.
- Turn off the gas in your home until someone can check it.
- If the power is out, find a battery-powered radio for updates.
- Avoid the beach (there could be a tsunami).
- Expect that aftershocks—usually smaller earthquakes—will occur.

TRAPPED IN A SINKING CAR!

IF A CAR BEGINS TO SINK IN A BODY OF WATER, THE VEHICLE HAS TURNED INTO A DEATH TRAP. WITH CUNNING AND QUICK ACTION, PEOPLE TRAPPED IN SINKING CARS CAN AVOID THIS GRISLY FATE, BUT WHEN PANIC SETS IN, HOW MANY PEOPLE ARE ABLE TO ACT SPEEDILY ENOUGH TO SAVE THEIR OWN LIVES?

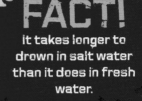

FACT!
It takes longer to drown in salt water than it does in fresh water.

Death due to drowning can take between three and four minutes, though the ideal time to rescue someone is within the first minute. The majority of people who are rescued from drowning but still require CPR either succumb to their trauma later or suffer brain damage.

LIVE OR DIE?

Your car veers off its path and barrels out of control through a rickety railing. With a great splash, it hits the water below, and you find yourself trapped inside your vehicle, quickly sinking into the darkness of the sea.

You have a narrow window of time to save yourself . . . and it's time to act!

OPTION #1

ATTEMPT TO OPEN THE CAR WINDOW AS QUICKLY AS POSSIBLE, TAKE OFF YOUR SEAT BELT, AND THEN STAY IN THE CAR UNTIL THE WATER RISES TO YOUR CHIN. THEN SWIM RAPIDLY TO THE SURFACE.

OPTION #2

FORCE THE DOOR OPEN, AND BEFORE THE WATER FILLS THE CAR, FREE YOURSELF FROM THE VEHICLE AND SWIM TO THE SURFACE.

OPTION #3

TAKE OFF YOUR SEAT BELT FIRST, OPEN THE CAR WINDOW NEXT, AND THEN STAY IN THE CAR UNTIL THE WATER RISES TO YOUR CHIN. THEN, SWIM RAPIDLY TO THE SURFACE.

SUCCESS! OPTION #1

The first priority is opening the window, ensuring an escape path. You want to avoid relying on the door, which might not open due to the pressure, so creating that opening is an essential first step. Unbuckling your seat belt is secondary to opening the window, because you will easily be able to remove the belt no matter how much water rises. Once there is enough water to completely submerge your body, you can swim free of the car and make your way toward the surface.

CAUTION! OPTION #2

There is a chance the door will open, but the physical threat to your body when attempting to squeeze through a car door under water pressure is great and may impede your ability to swim to the surface. In order to make it out alive, you must avoid injury at all costs.

DANGER! OPTION #3

While similar to the first method, prioritizing the seat belt over the window eats up time. If you are unable to open the window or door, you might have to resort to breaking the window. A flashlight or the seat's headrest may help, but this takes more time and energy and will waste precious oxygen that you won't have to spare!

Escaping such a grim fate will get your heart pumping and adrenaline racing, which can cause serious injuries to go unnoticed. No matter how you feel upon escaping the car, you should still head to the hospital to get checked out.

CPR, or cardiopulmonary resuscitation, can be used to help someone who has stopped breathing. The procedure is a combination of chest compressions and mouth-to-mouth breathing that even young kids can learn. CPR courses are taught in schools, at hospitals, and even in fire stations. Learning it can help save a person's life.

If a person stops breathing, severe brain damage or even death can occur in under eight minutes.

LIGHTNING STRIKES!

THE ODDS OF GETTING STRUCK BY LIGHTNING ARE INCREDIBLY LOW, BUT IT IS ALSO FOUR TIMES MORE LIKELY THAN WINNING THE LOTTERY. TAKING A CLOSER LOOK AT THE ODDS IS UNNERVING WHEN YOU REALIZE THAT THE LIKELIHOOD OF GETTING STRUCK IN YOUR LIFETIME IS ONE IN 12,000! IT'S NOT COMMON BY ANY STRETCH OF THE IMAGINATION, BUT IT'S STILL A GOOD IDEA TO KNOW HOW TO PROTECT YOURSELF.

FACT!

Lightning strikes occur upwards of 25 million times per year in the United States!

While worldwide estimates vary, in the United States there are between 40 and 50 deaths by lightning strike annually. Approximately 10 percent of strikes are fatal, though people who have experienced the brunt of this electrostatic discharge have reportedly felt its effects throughout their lives, including persistent migraines.

LIVE OR DIE?

You are outside, camping near a peaceful path in the woods when the sky darkens, thunder starts to rumble, and the sky flashes with lightning. You're surrounded by trees and you fear that walking back to your car, which is miles away, could put you in danger!

How will you avoid being struck by lightning?

OPTION #1

LIE FLAT ON THE GROUND.

OPTION #2

FIND A SMALLER GROUP OF TREES THAT ARE NEAR LARGE TREES, AND TAKE SHELTER THERE.

OPTION #3

CROUCH DOWN TO THE GROUND, MAKING YOURSELF AS SMALL AS POSSIBLE.

SUCCESS! OPTION #3

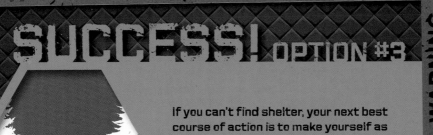

If you can't find shelter, your next best course of action is to make yourself as small as possible. Keep your head low, reducing your likelihood of being struck.

CAUTION! OPTION #2

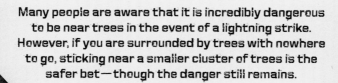

Many people are aware that it is incredibly dangerous to be near trees in the event of a lightning strike. However, if you are surrounded by trees with nowhere to go, sticking near a smaller cluster of trees is the safer bet—though the danger still remains.

DANGER! OPTION #1

Lying flat on the ground increases your chances of being struck, essentially spreading your body over multiple potential striking points.

Lightning can be seen as a much larger version of the spark you see during a static shock. It results when positive and negative charges in storm clouds equalizing themselves with a temporary discharge.

People say that lightning never strikes the same place twice, but that isn't true at all. In fact, lightning strikes the Empire State Building in New York multiple times every year.

MOUNTAIN LION ENCOUNTER!

MOUNTAIN LIONS—ALSO KNOWN AS COUGARS, PANTHERS, PUMAS, AND PROBABLY MORE NAMES THAN ANY OTHER ANIMAL HAS—CAN BE FOUND IN MORE PLACES IN THE WESTERN HEMISPHERE THAN ANY OTHER MAMMAL OF ITS SIZE. AS HUMANS POPULATE MORE AREAS OF THIS TERRAIN, THE OVERLAP BETWEEN COUGAR TERRITORY AND NEW HOMES LEADS TO AN INCREASE IN ATTACKS.

FACT!

Mountain lions are territorial creatures and skilled hunters—a double-threat for those unfortunate enough to run across them in the wild.

Mountain lions have often been the victim of poachers. They have also suffered due to humans moving in on their habitat. These animals have experienced a great deal of territory loss at the hands of humans.

LIVE OR DIE?

During a walk through the wilderness, you find yourself mere yards away from a mountain lion. As it stares at you with golden eyes, you can feel your heart begin to pound in your chest. You know that if you panic, you will have already lost.

It's time to do something . . . but what?

OPTION #1

LOB STONES AND STICKS AT THE MOUNTAIN LION. SCREAM AND MAKE NOISE TO EXAGGERATE THE LEVEL OF THREAT YOU POSE.

OPTION #2

STAND STILL OR PLAY DEAD, SHOWING THE MOUNTAIN LION THAT YOU ARE NOT A THREAT.

OPTION #3

RUN.

SUCCESS! OPTION #1

Though engaging in a physical battle with the mountain lion may seem like a foolish move, your best bet is to make it seem as if you're not going to be easy prey. If you can demonstrate that you might be a dangerous adversary, the mountain lion will likely retreat.

DANGER! OPTION #2

Unlike a grizzly bear, a mountain lion is actually more likely to attack once it learns you aren't a threat! This course of action will result in the cougar realizing that you are easy prey—so watch out for that incoming bite to the neck.

DANGER! OPTION #3

Unless you have encountered a particularly lazy mountain lion who is already full, running away from this predator will guarantee only one thing: you will be caught.

Mountain lions are capable of powerful leaps, which can extend as far as 40 feet and as high as 15 feet.

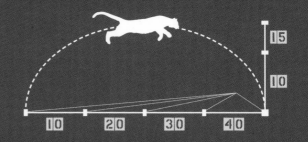

15
10

10   20   30   40

THE GO-TO ATTACK MOVE FOR THIS PREDATOR IS A SWIFT BITE TO THE NECK, CREATING INJURIES TO THE NECK, HEAD, AND SPINE THAT CAN BE FATAL.

SWARM OF BEES!

UNLESS YOU ARE ALLERGIC TO BEE STINGS, AN ENCOUNTER WITH A SINGLE BEE CAN BE UNPLEASANT BUT NOT ESPECIALLY DANGEROUS. HOWEVER, WHEN A COLONY OF BEES IS DISRUPTED AND A HUGE SWARM MADE UP OF COUNTLESS INSECTS ATTACKS, VICTIMS OF THEIR WRATH MAY FIND THEMSELVES IN A LIFE-OR-DEATH SITUATION. A SWARM OCCURS WHEN THE QUEEN BEE AND A LARGE GROUP OF WORKER AND DRONE BEES LEAVE A HIVE—AND IF YOU HAVE THE BAD LUCK OF BEING PRESENT WHEN THIS HAPPENS, YOU MIGHT FIND YOURSELF SURROUNDED BY UP TO TENS OF THOUSANDS OF BEES.

FACT!
Swarms offer opportunities for honeybees to reproduce.

60

Honeybee swarms are dangerous only if the swarm occurs near the nest, at which point they will act defensively. Unlike hornets, these insects will not attack unprovoked.

LIVE OR DIE?

While taking a casual stroll, you fall and, to your horror, disrupt a honeybee nest. As a seemingly endless number of bees pour out of the ruined nest, blocking your vision, you know that your peaceful stroll has just taken a treacherous turn.

What do you do to protect yourself?

OPTION #1

DIVE INTO NEARBY WATER TO ESCAPE THE ATTACKS.

OPTION #2

FEND OFF THE BEES WITH A STICK.

OPTION #3

RUN.

SUCCESS! OPTION #3

The only safe course of action is to run—and *keep* running. The bees will give chase, as they see you as a threat. Nothing but creating distance between yourself and the swarm will end well.

DANGER! OPTION #2

Fending off the bees alone will not work, as there can be up to 30,000 of them. No matter how skilled you are with a bat, no amount of baseball practice will enable you to stop an entire swarm with just a stick. If you have access to a stick *while* running, this method could work but it would be better to keep moving as fast as you can.

DANGER! OPTION #1

Diving into a body of water might seem like a way to make the bees go away, but as soon as you emerge, they will be hovering over the surface, waiting for you. What seemed like a surefire solution to this problem has instead trapped you!

After a honeybee stings you, its stinger remains in your skin, pumping venom into your wound. If you are stung by a single bee or a swarm, be sure to check yourself for stingers. The bees may be gone, but they just might have left you something to remember them by.

BEES SEEM LIKE ANNOYING PESTS, BUT THEY ACTUALLY PLAY AN IMPORTANT ROLE IN THE NATURAL WORLD.

- They spread pollen from plants and flowers to help them grow.
- They make tasty honey, which also has health benefits.
- Beeswax from their honeycombs is used in a variety of products, like candles, lip balm, and chewing gum.

HONEYBEE HIVES ARE DIVIDED INTO THREE TYPES OF BEES:

 QUEEN: Rules the hive by producing a chemical that controls the other bees. She lays all the eggs that grow the next generation of the hive.

 WORKERS: Female bees who gather food and protect the hive. These are usually the bees people see flying around.

 DRONES: Male bees who mate with the queen. Once winter comes, the drones are kicked out of the hive.

CROCODILE ATTACK!

CROCODILE ATTACKS HAVE BEEN THE SUBJECT OF URBAN LEGENDS, SO IT IS DIFFICULT TO GET A SENSE OF HOW OFTEN THESE CREATURES GO AFTER HUMANS. HOWEVER, IT IS CLEAR FROM THE INCIDENTS THAT HAVE BEEN REPORTED THAT CROCODILES HAVE ATTACKED HUMANS UNPROVOKED AND CAUSED FATALITIES. THOUGH THERE ARE MANY SPECIES OF CROCODILES THAT AREN'T CONSIDERED DANGEROUS TO HUMANS, SOME SPECIES—ESPECIALLY THE SALTWATER CROCODILE—HAVE BECOME INFAMOUS FOR THEIR AGGRESSION.

FACT!

Though they are often confused with alligators, crocodiles are differentiated by their longer head, their lighter coloring, the physical attributes of their teeth, and their aggression.

Crocodiles and dinosaurs lived at the same time, which suggests that crocodiles appeared on earth more than 240 million years ago. Crocodi are, in fact, closely related to both dinosaurs and birds. Their lifespan fluctuates depending on various factors, but they are known to live anywhere from 50 to 80 years.

LIVE OR DIE?

While you are relaxing, cooling your toes in the water after a hot day, a crocodile emerges nearby. You notice immediately, but it is already close, and will be upon you before you are able to withdraw your foot.

How do you protect yourself?

OPTION #1

ATTACK THE CROCODILE'S STOMACH.

OPTION #2

FLAIL YOUR ARMS AND LEGS WILDLY TO SCARE THE CROCODILE OFF.

OPTION #3

ATTACK THE CROCODILE'S FACE.

SUCCESS! OPTION #3

If a crocodile bites you, the quickest and most effective course of action is to attack its face, focusing your blows on its eyes and mouth. A nearby stick can be a useful weapon, but pointed attacks with your hands can also injure the animal enough to force it to release your foot from its jaws.

CAUTION! OPTION #1

It is true that the crocodile's stomach is more sensitive than the rest of its body, but you are being bitten and dragged underwater by a powerful reptile whose teeth are piercing your skin and flesh—you may have a hard time positioning yourself to hit its stomach. Even if you do so effectively, you may end up giving the crocodile a clear shot at your neck, which you want to avoid at all costs.

DANGER! OPTION #2

Flailing your limbs in the event of a crocodile attack will trigger the reptile's aggression, instigating an even nastier bite than you would've gotten initially. Calm and purposeful movements are more effective in escaping this one with your life.

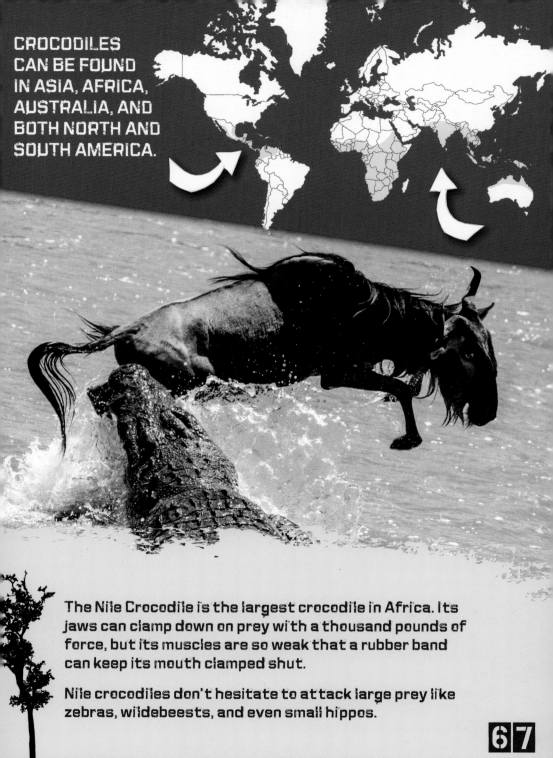

CROCODILES
CAN BE FOUND
IN ASIA, AFRICA,
AUSTRALIA, AND
BOTH NORTH AND
SOUTH AMERICA.

The Nile Crocodile is the largest crocodile in Africa. Its jaws can clamp down on prey with a thousand pounds of force, but its muscles are so weak that a rubber band can keep its mouth clamped shut.

Nile crocodiles don't hesitate to attack large prey like zebras, wildebeests, and even small hippos.

CAUGHT IN A RIP CURRENT!

IT CAN HAPPEN OUT OF NOWHERE. SEEMINGLY CALM WATERS CAN DECEIVE SWIMMERS, PULLING THEM AWAY FROM THE SHORE AND INTO DANGEROUS CURRENTS WITH LITTLE TO NO WARNING. RIP CURRENTS CAN BE FATAL IF THE SWIMMER ISN'T PREPARED, BUT SOMETIMES EVEN FORETHOUGHT AND CAREFUL ACTION FALL AWAY WHEN PANIC SETS IN.

WARNING RECURRING RIP CURRENTS NO LIFEGUARD ON DUTY

FACT!
Rip currents are the result of waves breaking against the shore.

A rip current is a narrow and strong flow of water moving along an otherwise calm surface. It forms near the shoreline and can quickly pull a person out into a deeper part of the ocean.

LIVE OR DIE?

During a fun day at the beach, you and your friends approach the shore. The water is calm here, so everyone begins to casually swim in the water. Before you can even scream, you feel a sudden, almost magnetic pull. As you are yanked away from the shore, you realize that you have been caught in a rip current. You have to act fast, or you will be swept back toward treacherous waters.

What do you do?

OPTION #1

SWIM PARALLEL TO THE SHORE TO PULL YOURSELF OUT OF THE RIP CURRENT.

OPTION #2

CALL FOR HELP.

OPTION #3

SWIM ALONG WITH THE RIP CURRENT TO BREAK FREE OF ITS PULL, AND THEN CIRCLE BACK AROUND TO SHORE.

SUCCESS! OPTION #1

Though they are powerful, rip currents are quite narrow. Swimming against the current will keep you in its path, but swimming parallel to the shore will move you successfully away from the current.

CAUTION! OPTION #2

Calling for help is advisable but not always possible. If your head goes under water, or if people are already being loud, using this tactic alone might not work. For best results, call for help while using Option #1 to attempt to free yourself from the rip current.

DANGER! OPTION #3

Swimming along with the current will take you farther away from shore, and away from the potential help of your friends. Reaching land is the goal here, so moving away from that goal will only worsen the situation.

RIP CURRENTS CAN MOVE FASTER THAN OLYMPIC SWIMMERS.

When you're in the ocean, always swim near a lifeguard.
That's your best chance of surviving any dangers in the water.

It's nearly impossible to see a rip current while you're swimming. Before you go in the water, you can check things out from an elevated position, like a sand dune, and see where the waves aren't breaking. If there are flat spots in the line of breaking waves or places where foam or sediment are being pulled away from the shoreline, avoid those spots when you get in the water.

70

PLANE CRASH!

YOUR CHANCES OF BEING KILLED IN AN AIRPLANE CRASH ARE APPROXIMATELY ONE IN 29,400,000. THOUGH THESE CHANCES SEEM IN YOUR FAVOR, THE NUMBER OF PLANE CRASHES AND THE CAUSES ASSOCIATED WITH THEM MIGHT STILL UNNERVE FREQUENT FLYERS. THIS RARE BUT TERRIFYING SITUATION SEEMS LIKE IT MEANS CERTAIN DEATH FOR EVERYONE ON BOARD, BUT BEING AWARE OF YOUR SURROUNDINGS AND KEEPING A DISASTER PLAN CAN GREATLY INCREASE YOUR CHANCE OF SURVIVAL.

FACT!

Crash tests show that passengers seated at the front of the plane are more vulnerable in the event of a crash than passengers in the back.

As technology advances, statistics change dramatically, so it is difficult to get a sense of how many aircrafts crash on average in a given year. There were 138 reported plane crashes in 2013 and 155 in 2012, with varying degrees of fatalities.

LIVE OR DIE?

You are a passenger on an airplane, and the worst possible scenario has occurred. A storm has caused an electrical failure on your plane, and the aircraft is going to crash.

What can you do to brace for impact and survive this horrifying turn of events?

OPTION #1

ONCE THE PLANE CRASH-LANDS, WAIT A MOMENT TO ASSESS THE SITUATION AND GAIN YOUR BEARINGS BEFORE ATTEMPTING TO EXIT THE CRAFT.

OPTION #2

GET YOUR LUGGAGE FROM THE OVERHEAD AND USE IT AS A SHIELD TO PROTECT YOURSELF FROM DEBRIS.

OPTION #3

LEAVE THE CRAFT AS SOON AS IT CRASH-LANDS, PUTTING IMMEDIATE DISTANCE BETWEEN YOURSELF AND THE AIRPLANE.

WARNING WARNING WARNING

SUCCESS! OPTION #3

You have chosen the best course of action. You should assess the situation and figure out where the plane may crash-land in the time leading up to the crash, preparing yourself with your flotation device and leaving behind any belongings. Once you have landed, escaping the plane and putting distance between yourself and the aircraft will keep you safe in the event of fire or an explosion.

CAUTION! OPTION #1

It might be impossible to get a sense of where the plane will crash, but waiting around once it has landed is risky. You might have a better grasp of the situation, but you have made yourself vulnerable to a possible explosion within the aircraft.

DANGER! OPTION #2

Getting up and attempting to wrest your luggage out of the overhead carrier will not make you safer—in fact, it will create a new danger. Keep your luggage where it is, grab onto your seat, and brace for landing, because when the plane is freefalling through the air, your suitcase will not function as a shield—it will become debris.

According to scientists, the turbulence felt commonly during flights may increase up to 40 percent by 2050 as a result of growing levels of carbon dioxide. On the bright side, technological advances have made it nearly impossible today for turbulence to cause a plane crash.

BE PREPARED!

Even though the odds of being in a plane crash are slim, there are still thing you can do to prepare yourself in case of emergency:

- Dress comfortably for travel. Have proper shoes and clothing for the weather in case you're stranded.

- Read the safety card provided on the plane and listen to the flight attendants give their pre-flight safety speech.

- Keep your seatbelt on at all times.

- Book a seat within five rows of an exit for your best chance of a timely escape.

WOLVES!

THE GRAY WOLF—OR THE TIMBER WOLF—IS ONE OF THE MOST INTENSELY STUDIED ANIMALS. IT HAS CAPTURED THE FASCINATION OF SCHOLARS AND BIOLOGISTS AND HAS ALSO TAPPED INTO THE FEAR OF HUMANS. BEARING A CLOSE RESEMBLANCE TO THE DOGS WE KEEP AS BELOVED PETS, THESE DANGEROUS CANINES TRAVEL IN PACKS AND WILL ACT OUT VIOLENTLY IF THEY FEEL THREATENED.

FACT!

As evidenced by the prevalence of wolf packs, wolves are social animals and will complete all of their daily activities in the company of other wolves.

Each pack has its own complicated hierarchy of dominance, most commonly with an alpha male and an alpha female, often a breeding pair, ranked the highest in the group. All of the wolves play different roles in the pack based on their ranking or associations with other pack members.

LIVE OR DIE?

While walking in the woods, you see what you initially believe to be a dog. Without thinking, you approach. Suddenly, this creature is joined by another . . . and another . . . and another . . . and just as quickly as you approached, you realize that you have encountered not just a wolf but a wolf pack.

With more and more of these feared canines gathering in front of you, prepared to defend their territory, what can you do to safely escape?

OPTION #1

STARE THE WOLVES DOWN TO SHOW THEM THAT YOU ARE A THREAT.

OPTION #2

RUN!

OPTION #3

BACK AWAY SLOWLY.

SUCCESS! OPTION #3

One of the only effective ways to diffuse the situation would be to back away slowly, leaving the wolves and their territory behind. If this fails, another course of action would be to hit the wolves with rocks from afar, though this also risks agitating them. A combination of these two methods, slowly retreating while gathering sticks and stones to use as weapons, would be most successful.

DANGER! OPTION #1

Wolves will often see a direct stare as a challenge, and will rise to meet that challenge. There are ways to scare off the wolves without egging them on, but this is not it.

DANGER! OPTION #2

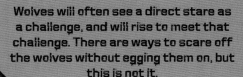

Once wolves sees their prey run, they hop into immediate action and will work together to catch you. Though your gut instinct might be to get away as quickly as possible, all you're doing is giving the wolves something to chase. Very, very briefly.

WARNING

WOLF PACKS GENERALLY CONSIST OF UP TO 10 WOLVES, THOUGH THERE HAVE BEEN PACKS WITH OVER 40 MEMBERS.

POSITIONS IN A WOLF PACK INCLUDE:

ALPHA: Leader of the pack, usually the largest wolf who commands respect.

BETA: Helps the Alpha lead the hunt; a second-in-command.

SIGMA & SELSA: Members of the hunting party that don't hold much respect in the pack.

DELTA & GAMMA: Hunters that tend to be the eldest of the pups.

EPSILON: Non-ranking members of the pack; they don't do much, but are still respected.

ZETA: A "beginners" rank in the pack; most will graduate to another level.

IOTA: Weaker members of the pack, including pups that just became adults. Also the rank for disruptive wolves.

OMEGA: Troublemakers; the least respected members of the pack.

CAUGHT IN A FLASH FLOOD!

WHEN RIVER BLOCKAGE, SUCH AS A MAN-MADE DAM OR A NATURALLY OCCURRING OBSTRUCTION, GIVES WAY TO THE PRESSURE OF THE WATER, A FLASH FLOOD OCCURS. WHILE ANY FLOOD CAN CAUSE IMMENSE DAMAGE AND EVEN FATALITIES, THE DANGEROUS PHENOMENA KNOWN AS FLASH FLOODS ARE ESPECIALLY DIFFICULT TO PREPARE FOR BECAUSE OF THEIR SPONTANEOUS NATURE, WHICH MAKES THEM THE MOST COMMON WATER-RELATED CAUSE OF DEATH IN THE UNITED STATES.

FACT!

Flash floods can occur as a result of other severe storms, as well as from meltwater, and can be distinguished from a standard flood because of the more limited timescale in which the water accumulates.

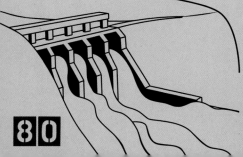

Floods have been known to damage land, property, bridges, roads, sewer systems, and power grids, sometimes leaving affected areas contaminated with dangerous substances even after the build-up of water diminishes.

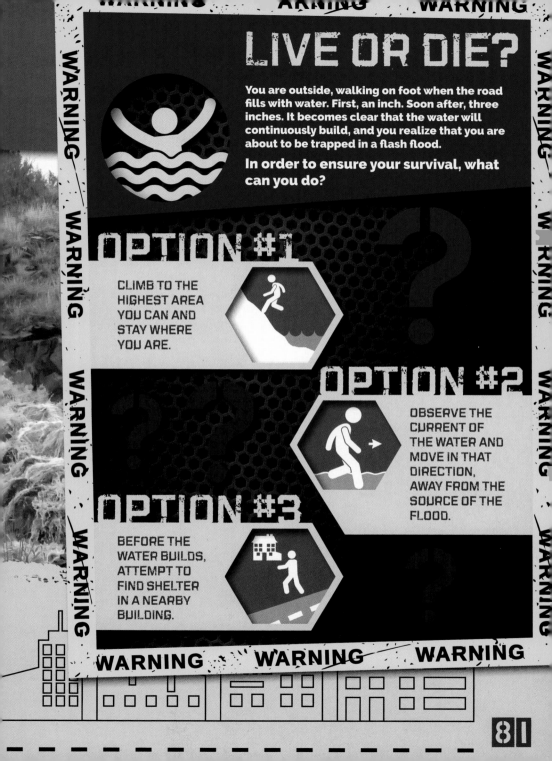

SUCCESS! OPTION #1

Though there is no way to completely guarantee your safety if you are stuck outside in a flash flood, you have chosen the most effective method of survival. If you can climb to the highest possible area, you lessen your chances of being swept up by the flood.

CAUTION! OPTION #3

While you are correct in thinking you would be safer indoors, walking through the beginnings of the flash flood is dangerous. Even mere inches of water could have the power to sweep you off your feet, and the speed at which the water rises makes this a risky choice.

DANGER! OPTION #2

Even if you are able to observe the direction of the water, you can't outrun a flash flood. Attempting to do so rather than seeking shelter or higher ground is your worst course of action.

Just because it's not raining where you are doesn't mean you're safe from a flash flood. If you're walking in a canyon that is prone to flooding, rain at a higher elevation can send water your way.

Avoid walking in canyons with walls that have water stains or debris lines from past flooding. There's a good chance they could flood again.

SOME OF THE DEADLIEST FLASH FLOODS IN THE UNITED STATES:

1889: Johnstown Flood, Pennsylvania - more than 2,200 people dead.
1903: Heppner Flood, Oregon - 247 dead.
1938: Los Angeles Flood, California - 115 dead.
1969: Nelson County Flood, Virginia - 123 dead.
1972: Black Hills/Rapid City Flood, South Dakota - 238 dead.
1976: Big Thompson River Flood, Colorado - 143 dead.

JELLYFISH STING!

JELLYFISH ARE COMMONLY FOUND ON BEACHES. WHILE THEIR STING CAN BE PAINFUL, THEY AREN'T OFTEN SEEN AS DEADLY CREATURES. MOST SPECIES ARE RELATIVELY HARMLESS, BUT THE BOX JELLYFISH HAS BEEN CALLED THE WORLD'S MOST VENOMOUS CREATURE, BEATING OUT THE KING COBRA, DEATH STALKER SCORPION, AND BRAZILIAN WANDERING SPIDER FOR THIS FEARSOME DISTINCTION. FATALITIES ASSOCIATED WITH THE BOX JELLYFISH HAVE OCCURRED IN AUSTRALIA AND THE PHILIPPINES, CEMENTING THE CREATURE'S RANK ON THIS LIST OF INFAMY.

FACT!

Despite their name, jellyfish are not actually fish. Rather, they are classified as cnidaria.

Jellyfish have tiny barbs on their tentacles that can easily pierce skin, injecting victims with venom. This can create a burning sensation and a rash, which can be quite painful even if the sting isn't fatal.

LIVE OR DIE?

While swimming, you have been stung by the most venomous creature in the world: a box jellyfish. You are alone and panicking, but you know that you have to act now if you wish to survive. After calling 911, you are left waiting.

In the time between the sting and the arrival of emergency medical help, what can you do to better your chances of survival?

OPTION #1

CREATE AN INCISION IN THE SKIN OF THE AFFECTED AREA TO BLEED OUT THE VENOM.

OPTION #2

APPLY VINEGAR TO THE STUNG AREA, FOLLOWED BY A COMPRESSION BANDAGE.

OPTION #3

REMOVE THE REMAINING STINGERS WITH YOUR FINGERS AND THEN APPLY A COMPRESSION BANDAGE.

SUCCESS! OPTION #2

Your preparation has paid off! If you have vinegar on hand, applying it to the location of the sting for over 30 seconds will render the venomous barbs inactive. Once you do this, isolate the stung areas with a compression bandage and wait for your ambulance to arrive.

CAUTION! OPTION #3

If you have not come prepared with vinegar in the event of a box jellyfish sting, your next best option is to manually remove the stingers. This can hurt your other hand, which is a risk, but dislodging these venomous barbs is necessary for survival.

DANGER! OPTION #1

Cutting the wound will do nothing to remove the venom and may increase your chances of going into shock.

WARNING WARNING WARNING WARNING

A BLOOM OF JELLYFISH, A SMACK OF JELLYFISH, A SWARM OF JELLYFISH; ALL OF THESE PHRASES ARE USED TO DESCRIBE A GROUP OF JELLYFISH.

Some types of jellyfish glow in the dark as a way of attracting prey or frightening off predators.

SOME PEOPLE BELIEVE THAT PEEING ON A JELLYFISH STING WILL MAKE THE PAIN GO AWAY, BUT THERE'S NO TRUTH TO THAT AT ALL.

CAUGHT IN A
BLIZZARD!

A TERRAIN COVERED IN THICK SNOW AND GLISTENING ICE IS A BEAUTIFUL SIGHT FROM AFAR. THIS PICTURESQUE SCENE CAN TURN NIGHTMARISH, THOUGH, IF YOU FIND YOURSELF TRAPPED OUTSIDE IN FREEZING TEMPERATURES AS A SNOWSTORM BUILDS AROUND YOU WITH NO SIGN OF SHELTER IN SIGHT. THERE ARE MANY WAYS THAT EXTREME WINTER CONDITIONS CAN LEAD TO FATALITIES, INCLUDING HYPOTHERMIA, CAR CRASHES, FROSTBITE, OR HEART ATTACKS DUE TO THE COLD.

FACT!

Not all snowstorms are blizzards. A blizzard is characterized by winds of at least 35 miles per hour that are sustained for upwards of three hours, creating low visibility.

Statistics show that an average of 10.7 blizzards occur annually in the United States, with numbers varying greatly each year. Some years have as little as a single blizzard, while other years are afflicted by over 20.

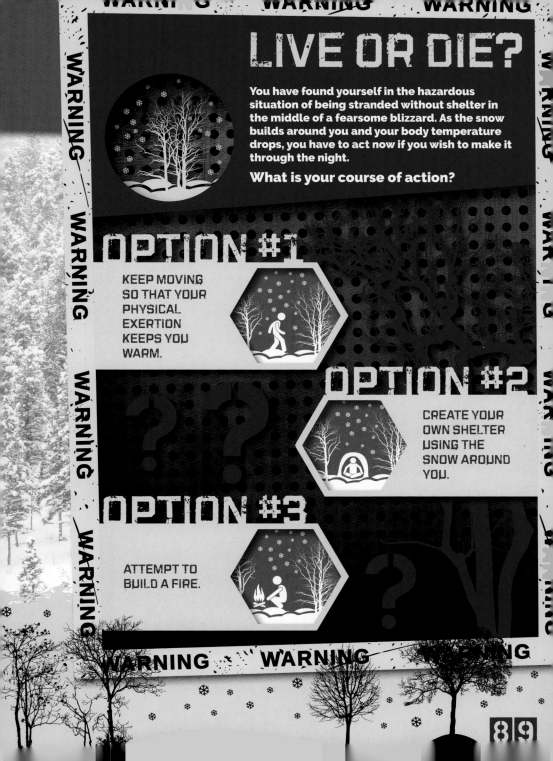

LIVE OR DIE?

You have found yourself in the hazardous situation of being stranded without shelter in the middle of a fearsome blizzard. As the snow builds around you and your body temperature drops, you have to act now if you wish to make it through the night.

What is your course of action?

OPTION #1

KEEP MOVING SO THAT YOUR PHYSICAL EXERTION KEEPS YOU WARM.

OPTION #2

CREATE YOUR OWN SHELTER USING THE SNOW AROUND YOU.

OPTION #3

ATTEMPT TO BUILD A FIRE.

SUCCESS! OPTION #2

If you are unable to find shelter, using the snow around you to create it is the safest option. If you can create an igloo, you will still be cold, but your chances of survival are much higher than if you remain outside, exposed to the elements.

CAUTION! OPTION #3

A successfully built fire would indeed help you survive, but your chances of being able to kindle the fire in the cold and wet environment of the blizzard are low. First and foremost, find shelter before worrying about attempting this course of action unless you are quickly able to produce dry wood.

DANGER! OPTION #1

Exercising lightly to keep your body warm will help you, but if you exert yourself enough to work up a sweat, you have increased your chances of succumbing to hypothermia.

WARNING   WARNING   WARNING

Nor'easters are blizzards that occur on the East Coast of the United States. When a storm stalls over the coastline along the Atlantic Ocean, it can stick around for more than 24 hours and dump a huge amount of snow.

Snowstorms occur when cold and dry air mingles with moist and warm air, creating a cold front.

IF YOU GET STUCK IN A CAR DURING A BLIZZARD, STAY INSIDE UNTIL THE STORM PASSES. IT'S GOOD TO KEEP A BLANKET IN THE CAR FOR JUST SUCH EMERGENCIES.

TSUNAMI!

WHILE EARTHQUAKES, LANDSLIDES, AND VOLCANIC ERUPTIONS ARE INCREDIBLY DANGEROUS BY THEMSELVES, EACH OF THESE NATURAL DISASTERS CAN TRIGGER A GIGANTIC WAVE KNOWN AS A TSUNAMI. TSUNAMIS HAVE CAUSED DEVASTATION WORLDWIDE, WITH SOME INDIVIDUAL EVENTS, LIKE THE INDIAN OCEAN TSUNAMI IN 2004, LEADING TO THE DEATHS OF APPROXIMATELY 200,000 PEOPLE.

FACT!

"Tsunami" is the Japanese word for "harbor wave."

Tsunamis were previously referred to as "tidal waves," but that term is rejected by modern science because these waves have nothing to do with the tide. They are, however, referred to as seismic sea waves.

LIVE OR DIE?

You have received word that your area is about to be hit by a tsunami. Panic ensues and people are attempting to evacuate, but the roads are beginning to get clogged and time is running out.

As the first wave is expected shortly, how can you best ensure your survival?

 HOLD ONTO A FLOTATION DEVICE.

OPTION #2

CLIMB TO HIGH GROUND OR, IF THAT IS IMPOSSIBLE, THE TOP OF A TALL TREE.

OPTION #3

 DRIVE AWAY FROM THE AFFECTED AREA IN HOPES OF BEATING THE FLOOD.

WARNING WARNING WARNING

SUCCESS! OPTION #2

While none of these courses of action are perfect on their own, and each offers its own possible perils, getting to the highest possible location is your best bet. Staying on solid ground is preferable to climbing a tree, but if your area is mostly level and climbing to the top of a tree is the only way to remove yourself from the ground, then that may be your safest course of action.

CAUTION! OPTION #1

Holding onto a floatation device is smart, but it would be unwise to rely on this device and wait for the wave to hit. While you can still survive, the chance that the force of the tsunami will rip the floatation device from your grasp is high. If you are able to carry this object with you to higher ground or up into a tree, combining this method with Option #2, you will be about as prepared for this tsunami as you can possibly get.

DANGER! OPTION #3

Though evacuation would be the best option if you had time, the fact that the roads are already clogged leaves people in their cars vulnerable to the tsunami. Unless you are absolutely sure you can safely navigate away from the affected area, your attempt at escape might actually ensure your demise.

Though evacuation is sometimes not possible, scientists are able to predict the time of arrival for tsunamis around the world based on the location and timing of earthquakes. However, earthquakes themselves cannot be predicted, so even with the accuracy of these scientific estimations, affected areas are often left vulnerable.

WARNING SIGNS

Signals that a tsunami is coming include earthquake; when the sea suddenly pulls far back from the shore; and when animals start behaving oddly or fleeing the area.

TSUNAMI
EVACUATION
ROUTE

AREAS IN THE UNITED STATES MOST AT RISK FOR TSUNAMIS INCLUDE HAWAII, ALASKA, WASHINGTON, OREGON, AND CALIFORNIA.

Brimming with creative inspiration, how-to projects and useful information to enrich your everyday life, Quarto Knows is a favorite destination for those pursing their interests and passions. Visit our site and dig deeper with our books into your area of interest: Quarto Creates, Quarto Cooks, Quarto Homes, Quarto Lives, Quarto Drives, Quarto Explores, Quarto Gifts, or Quarto Kids.

© 2017 Quarto Publishing Group USA Inc.

First Published in 2016 by becker&mayer, an imprint of The Quarto Group.
400 First Avenue North, Suite 400, Minneapolis, MN 55401, USA.
T (612) 344-8100 F (612) 344-8692 www.QuartoKnows.com

If you have questions or comments about this product, please visit www.beckermayer.com

Author: Pat Shand
Designer: Scott Richardson
Editor: Paul Ruditis
Photo research: Farley Bookout
Production coordinator: Cindy Curren

Printed & manufactured in Shenzhen, China June 2017

ISBN: 978-1-60380-405-9

16858

Image Credits:
pg 4: ©Scott E Read/ Shutterstock.com, pg 7: ©Ewais/ Shutterstock.com, pg 8: ©Zastolskiy Victor/ Shutterstock.com, pg 11: ©ellepistock/ Shutterstock.com, pg 12: ©Lysogor Roman/ Shutterstock.com, pg 15: ©scattoselvaggio/ Shutterstock.com, pg 16: ©Maria Dryfhout/ Shutterstock.com, pg 18: ©Leo Francini / Alamy Stock Photo pg 20: ©MISHELLA/ Shutterstock.com, pg 23: ©Suzanne Tucker/ Shutterstock.com, pg 24: ©Mark Williamson, pg 27: ©Roland Liptak / Alamy Stock Photo, pg 28: ©Dubrovskiy Vladimir/ Shutterstock.com, pg 31: ©Mathias Boman/ Shutterstock.com, pg 32: ©Martin Prochazkacz/ Shutterstock.com, pg 37: ©OmaPhoto/ Shutterstock.com, pg 39: ©Shane Pinder / Alamy Stock Photo, pg 40: ©Jauhien Krajko/ Shutterstock.com, pg 43: ©louise murray / Alamy Stock Photo, pg 44: ©Kawin Ounprasertsuk/ Shutterstock.com, pg 47: ©Photo by Frank Scherschel/The LIFE Picture Collection/Getty Images, pg 48: ©Odishev/ Shutterstock.com, pg 51: ©Sabina Zak/ Shutterstock.com, pg 52: ©Volker Schnaebele/ Shutterstock.com, pg 55: ©Dennis Hallinan / Alamy Stock Photo pg 56: ©Warren Metcalf/ Shutterstock.com, pg 59: ©Suha Derbent/ Shutterstock.com, pg 60: ©Darios/ Shutterstock.com, pg 63: ©Jim Nelson/ Shutterstock.com, pg 64: ©PROSIGN/ Shutterstock.com, pg 67: ©Sergey Uryadnikov/ Shutterstock.com, pg 68: ©Sundry Photography/ Shutterstock.com, pg 71: ©Suzanne Tucker/ Shutterstock.com, pg 72: ©Kamenetskiy Konstantin/ Shutterstock.com, pg 75: ©Naris Vachiranantavat/ Shutterstock.com, pg 76: ©David Dirga/ Shutterstock.com, pg 79: ©Michael Roeder/ Shutterstock.com, pg 80: ©Shabina Lourdes Dalidd/ Shutterstock.com, pg 83: ©Galyna Andrushko/ Shutterstock.com, pg 84: ©KJB/ Shutterstock.com, pg 87: ©Ewais/ Shutterstock.com, pg 88: ©Kent Weakley/ Shutterstock.com, pg 91: ©AimoKinnas/ Shutterstock.com, pg 92: ©Kelly Headrick/ Shutterstock.com, pg 95: ©J.D.S/ Shutterstock.com.

All design elements from Shutterstock.com.